INSPIRATIONAL LIVES

JAMIE OLIVER
CAMPAIGNING CHEF

Liz Gogerly

WAYLAND

First published in 2010 by Wayland

Copyright © Wayland 2010

Wayland
338 Euston Road
London NW1 3BH

Wayland Australia
Level 17/207 Kent Street
Sydney, NSW 2000

Senior editor: Camilla Lloyd
Designer: Rob Walster
Picture researcher: Shelley Noronha

Acknowledgments: p. 9 Top Tip: *The Guardian*, 31 January 2009; p.16 Wow!: Ireland's *Sunday Tribune*, June 2007.

Picture acknowledgments: The author and publisher would like to thank the following for allowing their pictures to be reproduced in this publication: Cover: Topfoto.co.uk; © Rune Hellestad/Corbis: 5; Getty Images: 13; Film Magic/Getty Images: 24; Sony Music Archive/Getty Images: 8; Rex Features Ltd: 6, 7, 10, 11, 12, 14, 16, 18, 19, 20, 21, 22, 23, 25, 26, 27; Empics/Topfoto: 4; National Pictures/Topfoto: 9, 15, 29; PA Photos/Topfoto: 28; Topfoto: 17.

British Library Cataloguing in Publication Data:
Gogerly, Liz.
Jamie Oliver. - (Inspirational lives)
1. Oliver, Jamie, 1975-Juvenile literature.
2. Celebrity chefs-Great Britain-Biography--Juvenile literature. 3. Television personalities-Great Britain-Biography-Juvenile literature.
I. Title II. Series
641.5'092-dc22

ISBN: 978 0 7502 6268 2

Printed in China

Wayland is a division of Hachette Children's Books, an Hachette UK company.

www.hachette.co.uk

Contents

Cooking up a storm

Television chef Jamie Oliver is a well-known, friendly face. People enjoy his banter as he explains how to knock up a tasty, healthy meal. But, in 2005, something wiped the smile off Jamie's face.

As part of his television series *Jamie's School Dinners,* Jamie visited school kitchens and dining rooms around the country. He found that kids were being fed 'rubbish'. They ate too many chicken nuggets, chips and chocolate bars. Fruit and vegetables were hardly on the menu.

And, given the choice, most children didn't want the healthy option. During the **documentary,** a doctor told Jamie that she was seeing children who had been **constipated** for six weeks due to a diet of **processed foods.** Poor diet also affects behaviour and performance at school.

Since Jamie's School Dinners *more children are being offered free school meals.*

In the future it may even cause serious health problems. Jamie felt Britain's children deserved better. Jamie is rich and successful. He could have sat back and done nothing about the situation. Instead, he fought to change school dinners. He proved that he could create healthy school meals for the same price as a bag of crisps.

Jamie's turned his quest into a national campaign called Feed Me Better. Since his programme was aired the government, as a result of a **petition**, has introduced new **nutrient** standards for school meals.

Jamie and Jools take Daisy Boo and Poppy Honey to watch the premiere of Harry Potter and the Half Blood Prince.

WOW!

In 2006 Jamie met with Prime Minister Tony Blair at 10 Downing Street. Jamie delivered a petition for better school meals. Later, he sat down with the Prime Minister to discuss the changes.

The young tearaway

James Trevor Oliver was born on 27 May 1975 in Southend, England. His parents Trevor and Sally are a down-to-earth couple. They adore each other and surrounded Jamie and his younger sister Anna-Marie with their love. The Olivers dreamed of running their own pub in the Essex countryside. When Jamie was still a baby the family moved to The Cricketers, a country pub in the village of Clavering.

The pub became famous for its fresh hearty food and relaxed atmosphere. Young Jamie fondly remembers Sundays at the pub. That was the day his family sat down together and got stuck into a Sunday roast. Jamie often returns with the family for Sunday lunch.

Jamie reckons his Mum is the best cook in the world – especially roasts and puddings!

WOW!

Jamie admits he was a wild child and accident-prone. When he was little he thought he could fly. He tried flying down the stairs in his Superman pyjamas and knocked himself out!

Jamie's Mum and Dad have run The Cricketers for over 30 years.

"I'm sure everyone thought I was a spoiled brat ... I always had whatever trainers I wanted, and I can honestly say I earned every single penny. My old man never gave me handouts. Ever."

Trevor was a loving dad but he was firm. Young Jamie was well known for being a tearaway and playing tricks. He enjoyed mucking around outdoors, making dens and fishing with his mates.

Jamie helped out in the pub too but could be a pest. When he was about ten he let off a stink bomb in the bar. About seventy customers fled the pub and half of them didn't pay.

INSPIRATION

"My old man is a mega hero!" Jamie is proud of his father, Trevor. He told Jamie: "Sometimes it only takes a smile to brighten up a customer's day." Jamie Oliver

Tinkering in the kitchen

Growing up in a pub gave Jamie the opportunity to learn about cooking from an early age. His parents always encouraged him to have a go. Jamie's early memories include experimenting with food and creating plates of ashes. By the age of eight he was whisking up tasty omelettes. Friends often came back to the pub to feast on Jamie's creations.

Jamie also had a taste for good food. He liked to share his enjoyment with others. Once he brought some traveller boys back to the pub. He gave them smoked salmon dripping with lemon juice. Jamie got loads of enjoyment from just watching the boys gobble up his delicious snack.

Jamie lets off steam playing the drums with his band Scarlet Division.

None of Jamie's teachers thought Jamie would go far in life. He was mischievous and interrupted lessons. Part of the problem was he had **dyslexia** so he struggled with reading.

Many actors, artists and musicians battle with dyslexia but are highly talented. Jamie has proved that dyslexia is not an obstacle when it comes to becoming a successful chef. Jamie has said: "I'm dyslexic, and I hated school, and I dropped out as soon as I could... Actually, I felt like a bit of a loser as an adolescent...but then my parents began urging me to cook in the family restaurant..."

*Jamie is a big fan of using **organic** produce. In his television series* Jamie at Home, *he uses fresh herbs, locally grown vegetables and free-range animal products.*

TOP TIP

"Try and convince Mum and Dad to let you do it [cook]. Make a bit of a mess once a week. You know, get stuck in. If you really like food, there's nothing like getting a job in a local restaurant or pub. What I learned in my Dad's pub when I was working for my pocket money, I still use today."
Jamie Oliver

London calling

School was a struggle but Jamie made lots of friends. He also met his future wife Juliette Norton, otherwise known as Jools. When Jamie wasn't larking about at school he was learning skills in the kitchen. By the time he was fourteen he was helping to plate up 120 meals a night in the pub. He left school at sixteen with two GCSEs in art and geology. He enrolled at Westminster Catering College in London to train to become a chef.

Gourmet chef, Gennaro Contaldo won an award for his restaurant Passione in London in 2005.

The move to London meant being away from his family and apart from girlfriend, Jools. Jamie missed the countryside and felt homesick. Soon, the buzz of the **culinary** capital of Britain took hold of Jamie. He threw himself into learning the basics of catering. He spent time in different kitchens learning new skills.

Jamie found some of the reading and science difficult because of his dyslexia, but he never complained about the workload. He specialised in pasta and bread-baking. After college he spent time travelling in France to learn about its **cuisine**. On his return to London he took up an **apprenticeship** in the Neal Street Restaurant of Antonio Carluccio, one of the most admired Italian chefs in Britain.

When Jamie was in London he travelled by scooter.

INSPIRATION

Jamie worked with Gennaro Contaldo at the Neal Street Restaurant. Gennaro passed on his passion for pasta and bread-making to the bright-eyed Jamie. Jamie calls Gennaro his 'London Dad'. Even though Jamie is one of the most famous chefs in Britain he still speaks to Gennaro on the telephone every day.

TOP TIP

"It sounds a bit stuffy when you say it ... but education can really open doors for you, and even someone like me, who basically messes up at school, can get his life together if he gets on the right course."
Jamie Oliver

The big break

Jamie arrived in London at an exciting time in British Cuisine. The first gastro-pub opened in the capital in 1991. It offered fine food in the comfort of the good old British pub. Meanwhile, London chefs were taking food to new heights. In the recent past **nouvelle cuisine** had dominated top British restaurant menus.

Now cuisine from all over the world was being created in London. Jamie's first real job was as a **sous-chef** at the famous River Café. The restaurant was creating a stir with its simple Mediterranean-style food.

Jamie loved his job at the River Café.

In 1996 a camera crew was making a documentary about the River Café. Baby faced with messy blonde hair, Jamie stood out on film. He talked easily to the camera about what he was doing. He threw in cheeky **'mockney'** comments which made everyone laugh. Most of all, his love of food was infectious.

When the documentary was aired, it was Jamie who stole the show. A phone call from television producer Pat Llewellyn sealed his fate. She was looking for a TV chef who could pull in younger viewers, especially men. Jamie was to be the man she was looking for...

INSPIRATION

He is the River Café's most famous chef but Jamie admits that owner-cooks Ruth Rogers and Rose Gray were a great influence. At the River Café Jamie learned that you didn't need to play around with food if you had the best fresh ingredients.

Jamie attends a charity event for leukemia in 2004 with Ruth Rogers (second on right) and Rose Gray (far right).

The Naked Chef

Jamie was having such a great time at the River Café that he wasn't sure he wanted to do a television show. The BBC wasn't convinced this inexperienced young chef was the man for the job either. Luckily, producer Pat Llewellyn knew she was on to a winner!

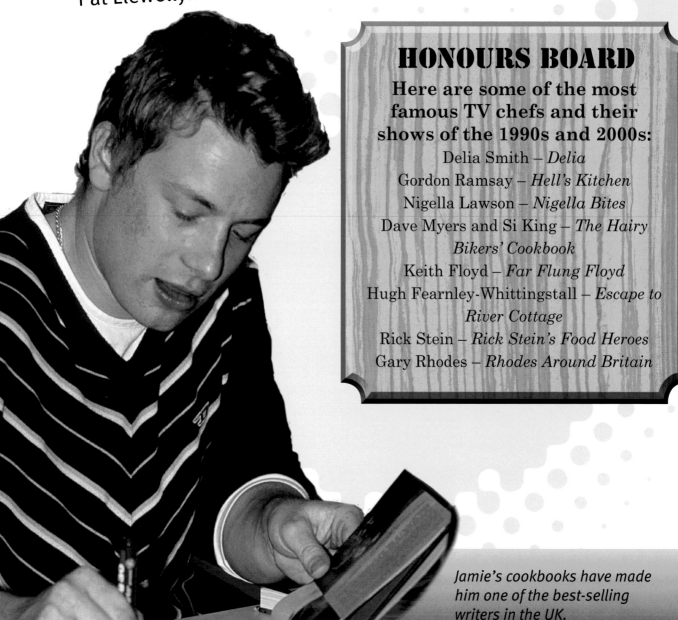

HONOURS BOARD

Here are some of the most famous TV chefs and their shows of the 1990s and 2000s:

Delia Smith – *Delia*

Gordon Ramsay – *Hell's Kitchen*

Nigella Lawson – *Nigella Bites*

Dave Myers and Si King – *The Hairy Bikers' Cookbook*

Keith Floyd – *Far Flung Floyd*

Hugh Fearnley-Whittingstall – *Escape to River Cottage*

Rick Stein – *Rick Stein's Food Heroes*

Gary Rhodes – *Rhodes Around Britain*

Jamie's cookbooks have made him one of the best-selling writers in the UK.

Jamie's first television series, *The Naked Chef*, was aired in the UK on BBC2 in 1999. Jamie said about the title of the series, "The name was supposed to be a reference to the food being stripped right down to the bare essentials. Not me ... I have hated the title from day one but it has been a great brand name."

The series was a hit, sometimes pulling in more than five million viewers. The show was as much about Jamie's life style as his cooking. There were scenes of him whizzing around London markets and shops on his scooter. Later, viewers watched him feasting with friends and family.

It was the scenes where Jamie cooked the food that inspired people to have a go themselves. "Jamie was a deliciously appetising ready-meal for TV: simply add liberal quantities of groovy tunes, whirling yoof camerawork, scooters, 'mates' and mockney geezer chat ..." Kathryn Flett, wrote in *The Observer* in July 2001.

Jamie returned with two more series of *The Naked Chef* in 2000 and 2001. The series turned Jamie into a household name and a millionaire by the age of 24.

In 1998, the supermarket, Sainsbury's, signed Jamie up to star in their TV adverts.

A day in the life of Jamie Oliver

Jamie worked as a sous-chef at River Café, which meant he was second-in-command running the kitchen. The sous-chef is in charge of cooking the food. The job involves everything from ensuring the kitchen is spotless, ordering stock, organising the kitchen staff to prepping and cooking the food.

It's a demanding job, which means being in the kitchen early in the morning and staying there until dinner is served. Jamie learned how to run a busy kitchen at River Café. This certainly set him up for the next stage in his career.

WOW!

"We [chefs] don't eat dinner. It's just impossible. From about 6.30 to 10.30 you're tasting, tasting, tasting, seeing your dishes on the menu. ... Going to the kitchen and wanting to taste what the customer is experiencing is crucial."
Gordon Ramsay, June 2007

Jamie loves using fresh ingredients and organic produce.

These days Jamie spends a lot of time promoting healthy eating.

In the past Jamie worked seven days a week. Now he is a father of three he tries to keep the weekends for his family. This isn't easy with so many business interests.

TV programmes such as *Jamie's American Road Trip* mean he has to be away from home. When he isn't filming, he's writing and promoting cookbooks or managing his string of restaurants and shops. There is a *Jamie Magazine* to run too. No day is like any other for Jamie Oliver but he isn't about to stop what he's doing: "I could have retired 10 years ago, at 24 … if I'm clever enough and embrace good people, we can do some really good stuff. You've got to keep creating."

WOW!

Jamie would invite many of his favourite bands to his dream dinner party. Round the table there'd be the Rolling Stones, U2, the Cure, Stone Roses and Oasis.

Oliver's Twist

Jamie's relationship with Jools is always in the news. In the early days pictures of the glamorous young couple out on the town were often in the newspapers. On 24 June 2000 photos of Jamie and Jools' wedding day made the front pages. Over the next few years the Olivers' new babies made the headlines. Jamie and Jools always wanted a big family. Their first daughter Poppy was born in 2002, Daisy arrived in 2003 with Petal following in 2009. The couple make no secret that they would like a boy, too.

Jamie and Jools married in Essex. Jamie was up at 5 am baking bread for the guests!

HONOURS BOARD

Here are some of Jamie's best-selling books:

The Naked Chef (1999)
The Return of the Naked Chef (2000)
Happy Days with the Naked Chef (2001)
Jamie's Kitchen (2002)
Jamie's Dinners: The Essential Family Cookbook (2006)
Jamie's Italy (2007)
Jamie at Home: Cook Your Way to the Good Life (2007)
Jamie's Ministry of Food: Anyone Can Learn to Cook in 24 Hours (2008)
Cook With Jamie: My Guide to Making You a Better Cook (2009)
Jamie's Red Nose Recipes (2009)
Jamie's America (2009)
Jamie's Food Revolution: Rediscover How to Cook Simple, Delicious, Affordable Meals (2009)

After *The Naked Chef* series in 2009, Jamie set up his own production company, Fresh One Productions. The company came up with a new series called *Oliver's Twist*. It was made especially for the international market. The series was shown in over 50 countries. Jamie was especially popular in Australia, Germany and Holland. Even the French, who pride themselves on their own cuisine, enjoyed his shows.

Jamie was also a hit in America and he's now one of the top chefs on the Food Channel. Jamie has not just been a success on screen. He has become the top-selling author of cookbooks in the UK. His books have also been translated into 23 languages.

WOW!

In 2001 Jamie went on the road with a live show. 'The Happy Days Live' tour included live cookery demonstrations with music and special effects.

A poster advertising a German musical called Das Jamie Oliver Dinner.

DAS JAMIE OLIVER DINNER

Ein kulinarisches Theater-Spektakel

Charity begins in the kitchen

Jamie Oliver wanted to think about how he could help other people and he decided to set up a charity. Jamie's idea was to set up a top-class restaurant where unemployed and disadvantaged kids could learn to be qualified chefs. The restaurant would be called Fifteen. The name came about because fifteen kids would be chosen each year to train in the restaurant kitchens.

In 2002 the public got to see how Jamie founded Fifteen in a series called *Jamie's Kitchen*. This wasn't a cookery show, it was **reality drama**. Working with disadvantaged teenagers was no easy business.

Many recruits didn't turn up for training and were useless in the kitchen. Sometimes Jamie got angry and shouted because he was really rooting for these kids.

The ultra-modern Fifteen restaurant in London.

Fifteen Amsterdam was opened in December 2004. In 2006 Fifteen Newquay and Fifteen Melbourne were launched. Many people are asking where the next restaurant will be!

The documentary also showed Jamie panicking about going over budget. He had invested a lot of his own money in the project and he was worried about losing his home.

Fifteen Restaurant opened in London in November 2002. Celebrities like Brad Pitt and Jennifer Anniston were amongst the first customers. The restaurant is popular but has its critics. Jamie must have done something right because Fifteen restaurants are opening all over the world. And, many of the people who trained at Fifteen have top jobs in the catering industry.

Jamie celebrates with recent graduates from Fifteen Newquay.

WOW!

When Jamie cooked dinner for President Obama in 2009 he was joined by graduates from Fifteen. Chefs included Ben Arthur, a graduate from 2003, who now works with Theo Randall at the Intercontinental; Dennis Duncanson a graduate from 2004, who is now sous-chef at Jamie's Italian in Kingston.

What Jamie did next

Some people criticised Jamie for not wearing a tie when he received his MBE in 2003.

"At 28, I think I am probably the youngest person receiving an award today ... I thought I was a bit too young to receive an honour."

In October 2003 Jamie was made a MBE (Member of the Order of the British Empire), an award which is given for achievement or service in and to the community. Later that year Jamie was on the television in *Return to Jamie's Kitchen* to catch up with what was happening at Fifteen.

The public had to wait until 2005 to see Jamie on television again. This time, it was School Dinners (see pages 6–7). In School Dinners he overhauled the school lunches served up at a secondary school in London. He swapped kids' favourites such as burgers and chips for pasta

HONOURS BOARD
What Jamie would take with him to a desert island:

1. A nice sharp knife
2. A good pan
3. A load of spices which I'd plant so I could have them fresh
4. A lifetime supply of extra virgin olive oil
5. A fishing rod so I could catch my own fish

dishes and salads. "At first I didn't like the vegetables," said 10-year-old pupil Ayten Manyera. "Now I do. I have lots more energy." The teachers noticed the difference too with many of the children performing much better.

In 2005 Jamie turned 30. After School Dinners he needed a break. He wanted to get back to where it all began for him. In his next television programme Jamie's Great Italian Escape he toured around Italy in his VW campervan. The whole experience reminded him why he loved food and cooking so much. In his next programme, *Jamie at Home* (shown in 2007) he extended his love of food to the garden. In this series Jamie made tasty food using fresh ingredients grown in his own vegetable patch.

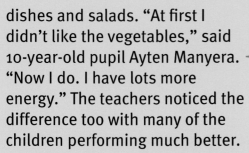

INSPIRATION

"It's my second year of growing my vegetable patch and I love it. That has given me such a lot of inspiration, a different inspiration than I had from walking around a market or meeting beautiful producers, or having parties or occasions. I think inspiration is around every corner." Jamie Oliver

Jamie dressed up in a fat suit to promote Jamie's Return to School Dinners in 2006!

Food fights

In 2008 the feisty foodie was back on the campaign trail. *Jamie's Fowl Dinners* was a hard-hitting documentary about the **poultry industry** in Britain. Jamie showed why supermarkets are able to offer cheap chicken. At the time, most British chickens were raised in large, windowless, overcrowded sheds. They were fattened quickly. As they grew they had less space to move.

Jamie believed that people should see how these birds were treated. People would then be able to make their own informed choices about buying chickens. Jamie wasn't suggesting that everyone ate organic chicken because that would be expensive. But, he was asking people to stop eating **battery-reared** hens and eggs. After the programme the sales of free-range or organic chicken went up by 50 per cent!

TOP TIP

"The biggest fact about cooking is that you do not have to be rich to eat well. All the best cooking in the world is from peasant culture and all those really cheap bits of meat like chicken drumsticks are fantastic to cook with and they don't break the bank."
Jamie Oliver

Jamie promoting his 2008 book, Ministry of Food.

Jamie's Italian in Oxford. The menu includes food prepared with the best fresh ingredients.

The next stop for Jamie was trying to change people's eating habits. He was concerned that many people did not know how to cook. In the past, family and friends had passed on what they knew in the kitchen. In his 2009 documentary, *Jamie's Ministry of Food,* he showed a group of people how to cook simple meals from scratch. Sales of the book, *Jamie's Ministry of Food,* made Jamie into the top-selling author in the UK in 2008.

WOW!

In 2008 Jamie launched a new chain of Italian restaurants, simply called Jamie's Italian. To date restaurants have opened in Oxford, Bath, Kingston, Brighton, Canary Wharf and Guildford.

Jamie conquers America

In April 2009 Jamie was back at 10 Downing Street, home to Prime Minister Gordon Brown. This time Jamie was in the kitchen creating "probably the most important meal I've ever cooked." Gordon Brown was hosting a dinner for the world heads of state at the **G20 Summit**. Amongst the guests were the President of the United States Barack Obama and his wife Michelle. Jamie wanted a menu that showed off the best of British food (see below).

Jamie was thrilled to be introduced to Barack and Michelle Obama at the summit.

HONOURS BOARD

A menu fit for the president:

Starter: Organic Scottish salmon with samphire and sea kale, and a selection of vegetables from Sussex, Surrey and Kent.

Main: Slow-roasted shoulder of Elwy Valley lamb with Jersey Royals, wild mushrooms and mint sauce.

Dessert: Bakewell tart and custard.

Vegetarian: Goat's cheese starter, followed by lovage and potato dumplings.

In 2009 Jamie filmed two series that focused on America. First to hit the television screens was *Jamie's American Road Trip*. Jamie found that American food isn't just burgers and fast food. Immigrants from all over the world have brought their own feasts and flavours to the country. In the backstreets of New York he shared ceviche (a seafood dish) with Peruvians. In Arizona he sampled native American food with the **Navajo**.

WOW!

In 2009 Jamie started a chain of food stores called Recipease. Two branches opened in London and Brighton. The shops sell organic ingredients, freshly cooked meals and kitchen equipment. Customers can also learn to cook with the help of professional chefs.

When Jamie visited Los Angeles he went in search of authentic Mexican food. Later in 2009 Jamie began filming his first show, *Jamie Oliver's Food Revolution*, for the major US network, ABC. Huntingdon, West Virginia has been declared America's 'fattest city'. Jamie was on a mission to help the residents of Huntingdon stop eating fast food and start cooking healthy meals.

Jamie dressed up as members of the 1970s band, Village People, for the TV programme Jamie's American Road Trip.

The impact of Jamie Oliver

Jamie scooted into our lives as the Naked Chef in 1999. In the early days Jamie charmed us with his no-nonsense approach to cooking. He could mix up a **marinade** for meat in moments. He squished the juice out of lemons using his bare hands. Everything in a frying pan was shaken not stirred. It was an exciting approach to cookery which earned him lots of young fans.

Jamie tackling unhealthy eating in the House of Commons (2008).

These days Jamie is much more than a celebrity chef. His reputation changed when he headed the campaign to improve school dinners. People were struck by his care for young people. They admired his determination to make changes. Some people even thought he should become a politician. Since *Jamie's School Dinners* he has championed the cause of battery chickens and British pork farmers. In his programme *Jamie's Ministry of Food* he tried to change unhealthy diets in Britain.

Jamie has the knack of making everything look fun and easy, and that includes making money. In fact, Jamie is a shrewd businessman. He was a millionaire by the age of 24. By 2009 he was believed to be worth more than £40 million, making him the 1,348th richest person in Britain (*Sunday Times* Rich List 2009). The Jamie Oliver brand is known around the world and continues to grow. Nobody knows what Jamie will do next but it's likely to cause a stir!

HONOURS BOARD

Jamie's television shows:
The Naked Chef (1999)
Return of the Naked Chef (2000)
Happy Days with the Naked Chef (2001)
Oliver's Twist (2002)
Jamie's Kitchen (2002)
Return to Jamie's Kitchen (2003)
Jamie's School Dinners (2005)
Jamie's Great Italian Escape (2005)
Jamie's Return to School Dinners (2006)
Jamie's Australian Kitchen (2006)
Jamie's Chef (2007)
Jamie at Home (2007)
Jamie at Home Christmas Special (2007)
Jamie's Fowl Dinners (2008)
Jamie's Ministry of Food (2008)
Jamie Cooks Christmas (2008)
Jamie Saves Our Bacon (2009)
Jamie's American Road Trip (2009)
Jamie's Family Christmas (2009)
Jamie Oliver's Food Revolutoin (2009-10)

Jamie has revealed his recipe for success: "I really, really do generally, first and foremost, make creative decisions based on what feels right, and anything monetary follows if it's good..."

Have you got what it takes to be a top chef? Try this!

1) Are you passionate about good food?
a) Yes, there's a whole world of food and flavours out there to discover.
b) Yes, I love tasty food.
c) I like food but I'm not into cooking.

2) Do you cook yourself?
a) Yes, if I'm not in the kitchen I've got my nose in recipe books.
b) Yes, I can fry an egg, boil pasta etc.
c) No, I can't even boil an egg.

3) When you eat something do you think about how you'd improve it?
a) Yes, always!
b) Yes, but I don't know much about cooking.
c) No, I know what I like and what I don't like.

4) Have you worked in a professional kitchen?
a) Yes, I have a part-time job in my local gastro-pub. I'm learning loads!
b) I've thought about getting a part-time job in a restaurant but I don't feel confident enough.
c) No, it looks like hard work to me.

5) Have you considered going to catering college?
a) Yes, I've looked into it and would like to go when I leave school.
b) Yes, but I'm not sure if I'd get in.
c) No way!

6) Chefs have to work unsociable hours; could you cope with that?
a) Yes, the buzz of the kitchen and learning about food would keep me going.
b) I'm not a morning person so I'm not sure how I'd handle early mornings AND late nights!
c) No – I'd like a nine to five job!

7) Are you self-disciplined, hardworking and dedicated to being in a hot, sweaty kitchen?
a) Yes, but that's not the only thing that being a top chef is about, it's also about having pride in what you're doing, creating gorgeous food and having a great time!
b) I think I am but I won't know until I try.
c) I'm self-disciplined but just not interested in cooking.

RESULTS

Mostly As: You have the makings of a chef. You have the enthusiasm and seem to be realistic about what the job entails. Good luck!

Mostly Bs: You have an interest in good food but is that enough for a professional career in catering? You should try and get a part-time job in a kitchen and find out if you're cut out for catering.

Mostly Cs: The food bug hasn't hit you yet. Why not try getting into the kitchen and see if cooking is as simple and fun as Jamie Oliver says?

Glossary

apprenticeship   A way of learning a profession on-the-job.

battery-reared   A system of rearing chickens. The birds are kept indoors, under strictly controlled and cramped conditions.

constipated   To have a medical condition called constipation. Poor diet can sometimes lead to faeces (poo) becoming hard and difficult to pass.

cuisine   A style of cooking often from a particular country or associated with certain chefs.

culinary   Something related to or connected with cooking.

documentary   A television programme that presents the facts about a given subject. This often involves showing real events and interviews with the people involved.

dyslexia   A condition which makes it difficult for a person to read and spell.

G20 Summit   A meeting of world leaders to discuss matters of international finance.

marinade   A mixture of oil, vinegar, herbs and spices in which meat or fish are soaked before cooking. This adds flavour and keeps food tender.

mockney   A word made from combining the words 'mock' and 'cockney.' A cockney is someone from a small area in London who has a distinct accent. Jamie Oliver was not born in London but he speaks with a Cockney accent and uses some cockney words - he's a 'mockney'!

Navajo   American Indian people who live in the states of New Mexico and Arizona.

nouvelle cuisine   A modern style of cookery. This style is famous for its attention to presentation. It's also known for its smaller than average portions.

nutrient   The nourishing part of the foods we eat; the part that provides the essential vitamins and minerals the human body requires to keep it healthy.

organic   Organic food is produced without the use of harmful chemicals, such as pesticides and fertilizers.

petition   This is a document requesting change that is signed by people in support of the proposed change.

poultry industry   The industry involved in selling the meat or eggs of chickens, turkeys, geese or ducks.

processed food   Food that has been treated with chemicals to make it taste or look a certain way, or to preserve it for longer.

reality drama   A television programme which closely follows the lives of real people and events.

sous-chef   The chef's assistant and second-in-command. There may be more than one sous-chef in a kitchen.

Index

INSPIRATIONAL LIVES

Contents of titles in series: